LEARN

MANDARIN
Chinese
WORDS

sun
太阳
(tài yáng)

swing
秋千
(qiū qiān)

clouds
云
(yún)

pond
池塘
(chí táng)

flower
花
(huā)

duck
鸭子
(yā zǐ)

BY M. J. YORK • ILLUSTRATED BY KATHLEEN PETELINSEK

The Child's World

Published by The Child's World®
1980 Lookout Drive • Mankato, MN 56003-1705
800-599-READ • www.childsworld.com

Acknowledgments
The Child's World®: Mary Berendes, Publishing Director
Translator: Weijun Chen, Chinese Language Instructor,
University of Oregon
The Design Lab: Design
Red Line Editorial: Editorial direction
Amnet: Production

ISBN 9781626873773
LCCN 2014930627

Printed in the United States of America
Mankato, MN
July, 2014
PA02217

ABOUT THE AUTHOR

M. J. York is a children's author and editor living in Minnesota. She loves learning about different people and places.

ABOUT THE ILLUSTRATOR

Kathleen Petelinsek loves to draw and paint. She also loves to travel to exotic countries where people speak foreign languages. She lives in Minnesota with her husband, two daughters, two dogs, a fluffy cat, and three chickens.

CONTENTS

Introduction to Chinese

More people live in China than any other country. And more people speak Chinese than any other language in the world! Forms of Chinese have been spoken for more than 3,000 years.

Mandarin Chinese is the most spoken form of Chinese. Two-thirds of the people in China speak it. Other forms of Chinese include Yue, Wu, Minbei, and many others.

Written Chinese does not have an alphabet with letters. Instead, it uses many characters. They stand for words or parts of words. People use a system called pinyin to write Chinese using Roman letters. Most pinyin letters are pronounced like English. But there are some differences:

c   pronounced like **ts** in ca**ts**

q   pronounced like **ch** in **ch**eap

x   pronounced like **sh** in **sh**ip

z   pronounced like **ds** in be**ds**

zh   pronounced like **j** in **J**ake

i	pronounced like **ee** in b**ee**
u	pronounced like **oo** in b**oo**k
ü	pronounced like **ee** with rounded lips.
ui	pronounced like **wei** in **wei**gh

Chinese is a tonal language. That means sounds spoken with a different pitch or tone of voice have different meanings. There are four tones in Mandarin Chinese:

1. *The first tone*: flat tone, such as ā in **mā** (妈, mother)
2. *The second tone*: rising tone, such as á in **má** (麻, numb)
3. *The third tone*: falling-rising tone, such as ǎ in **mǎ** (马, horse)
4. *The fourth tone*: falling tone, such as à in **mà** (骂, to scold)

My Home
我的家
(wǒ de jiā)

window
窗户
(chuāng hù)

bathroom
浴室
(yù shì)

lamp
台灯
(tái dēng)

bedroom
卧室
(wò shì)

television
电视机
(diàn shì jī)

kitchen
厨房
(chú fáng)

cat
猫
(māo)

living room
客厅
(kè tīng)

sofa
沙发
(shā fā)

chair
椅子
(yǐ zi)

table
桌子
(zhuō zi)

In the Morning
早晨/上午
(zăo chén /shàng wŭ)

dresser
衣橱
(yī chú)

clock
钟
(zhōng)

teddy bear
泰迪熊
(tài dí xióng)

doll
洋娃娃
(yáng wá wa)

pillow
枕头
(zhěn tou)

bed
床
(chuáng)

blanket
毯子
(tǎn zi)

At the Park
在公园
(zài gōng yuán)

Let's play!
让我们去玩吧!
(ràng wǒ mén qù wán ba!)

sky
天空
(tiān kōng)

friend (male)
朋友
(péng yǒu)

friend (female)
朋友
(péng yǒu)

bird
鸟
(niǎo)

soccer ball
足球
(zú qiú)

MORE USEFUL WORDS

game
游戏
(yóu xì)

sports
运动
(yùn dòng)

airplane
飞机
(fēi jī)

office
办公室
(bàn gōng shì)

building
大楼
(dà lóu)

bus
公交车
(gōng jiāo chē)

CITY BUS

MORE USEFUL WORDS

truck
卡车
(kǎ chē)

train
火车
(huǒ chē)

stop
停
(tíng)

go
走
(zǒu)

15

In the Store
在店里
(zài diàn lǐ)

My Birthday Party
我的生日聚会
(wǒ de shēng rì jù huì)

grandmother
(father's mother)
祖母
(zǔ mǔ)

grandfather
(mother's father)
外祖父
(wài zǔ fù)

I am six years old.
我六岁。
(wǒ liù suì.)

MORE USEFUL WORDS

older sister
姐姐
(jiě jie)

younger brother
弟弟
(dì di)

grandmother
(mother's mother)
外祖母
(wài zǔ mǔ)

grandfather
(father's father)
祖父
(zǔ fù)

cousin
(male, older)
表哥
(biǎo gē)

cousin
(female, younger)
表妹
(biǎo mèi)

aunt
(father's sister)
姑妈
(gū mā)

uncle
(mother's brother)
舅舅
(jiù jiu)

uncle
(father's older brother)
伯伯
(bó bo)

older brother
哥哥
(gē ge)

younger sister
妹妹
(mèi mei)

cake
蛋糕
(dàn gāo)

19

Time for Dinner
晚餐时
(wǎn cān shí)

bread
面包
(miàn bāo)

stove
炉子
(lú zi)

pot
锅
(guō)

I am hungry.
我饿了。
(wǒ è le.)

glass
玻璃杯
(bō li bēi)

rice
米饭
(mǐ fàn)

meat
肉
(ròu)

plate
盘子
(pán zi)

fork
叉子
(chā zi)

knife
刀
(dāo)

spoon
勺子
(sháo zi)

At Night
晚上
(wǎn shàng)

Good night!
晚安！
(wǎn ān!)

MORE USEFUL WORDS

Today is Friday!
今天是星期五！
(jīn tiān shì xīng qī wǔ!)

Yesterday was Thursday.
昨天是星期四。
(zuó tiān shì xīng qī sì.)

Tomorrow is Saturday.
明天是星期六。
(míng tiān shì xīng qī liù.)

bathtub
浴缸
(yù gāng)

I am tired!
我累了！
(wǒ lèi le!)

one 一 *(yī)*	eleven 十一 *(shí yī)*	thirty 三十 *(sān shi)*
two 二 *(èr)*	twelve 十二 *(shí èr)*	forty 四十 *(sì shí)*
three 三 *(sān)*	thirteen 十三 *(shí sān)*	fifty 五十 *(wǔ shi)*
four 四 *(sì)*	fourteen 十四 *(shí sì)*	sixty 六十 *(liù shi)*
five 五 *(wǔ)*	fifteen 十五 *(shí wǔ)*	seventy 七十 *(qī shí)*
six 六 *(liù)*	sixteen 十六 *(shí liù)*	eighty 八十 *(bā shí)*
seven 七 *(qī)*	seventeen 十七 *(shí qī)*	ninety 九十 *(jiǔ shi)*
eight 八 *(bā)*	eighteen 十八 *(shí bā)*	one hundred 一百 *(yī bǎi)*
nine 九 *(jiǔ)*	nineteen 十九 *(shí jiǔ)*	
ten 十 *(shi)*	twenty 二十 *(èr shi)*	

Yes
是的
(shì de)

No
不是
(bú shì)

winter
冬天
(dōng tiān)

spring
春天
(chūn tiān)

summer
夏天
(xià tiān)

fall
秋天
(qiū tiān)

good-bye!
再见！
(zài jiàn!)

January 一月 *(yī yuè)*	July 七月 *(qī yuè)*
February 二月 *(èr yuè)*	August 八月 *(bā yuè)*
March 三月 *(sān yuè)*	September 九月 *(jiǔ yuè)*
April 四月 *(sì yuè)*	October 十月 *(shí yuè)*
May 五月 *(wǔ yuè)*	November 十一月 *(shí yī yuè)*
June 六月 *(liù yuè)*	December 十二月 *(shí èr yuè)*